LES DAWSON'S CISSIE & ADA

Cover artwork by Tom Unwin

A RAZZAMATAZZ PUBLICATION

To Gary + Pam
Best wishes

[signature]

About the author

The day after Terry Ravenscroft threw in his mundane factory job to become a television comedy scriptwriter he was involved in a car accident which left him unable to turn his head. Since then he has never looked back.

Before they took him away he wrote scripts for Les Dawson, The Two Ronnies, Morecambe and Wise, Alas Smith and Jones, Not the Nine O'Clock News, Ken Dodd, Roy Hudd, and several others. He also wrote the award winning BBC radio series Star Terk Two.

Born in New Mills, Derbyshire, in 1938, he still lives there with his wife Delma and his mistress Divine Bottom (in his dreams).

Books by Terry Ravenscroft

AUTOBIOGRAPHY

STAIRLIFT TO HEAVEN
STAIRLIFT TO HEAVEN 2 - FURTHER UP THE
STAIRLIFT
STAIRLIFT TO HEAVEN 3 - ALMOST THERE
STAIRLIFT TO HEAVEN 4 - STILL HANGING ON

NOVELS

CAPTAIN'S DAY
FOOTBALL CRAZY
IT'S NOT CRICKET
JAMES BLOND - STOCKPORT IS TOO MUCH
I'M IN HEAVEN
INFLATABLE HUGH
THE RING OF THE LORD
SERIAL KILLER
JERRY'S
KIDNAPPED!

HUMOROUS CORRESPONDENCE

DEAR AIR 2000
DEAR COCA-COLA
DEAR PEPSI-COLA

SHORT STORIES AND OTHER BOOKS

THE RAZZAMATAZZ FUN EBOOK
ZEPHYR ZODIAC
SAWYER THE LAWYER
CALL ME A TAXI
GOOD OLD GEORGE

LES DAWSON'S CISSIE & ADA

Les Dawson's Cissie & Ada is a selection of some of the many scripts Cissie & Ada sketches I wrote for Les when I worked as his scriptwriter during the years 1978 to 1983, initially on three series of the BBC's *The Dawson Watch* and subsequently on three series of *The Les Dawson Show*. Les of course was Ada Shufflebottom. Ada's friend and neighbour Cissie Braithwaite was played by the wonderful Roy Barraclough, who later went on to star as Alex Gilroy in *Coronation Street*.

When I first met Les, to say I was in complete awe of the man would be a gross understatement: I was a still very wet behind the ears television scriptwriter whose only TV credits were for contributions to the 'news items' feature that topped and tailed *The Two Ronnies* show of fond memory, whereas Les was one of the biggest comedy stars in the country. What would I say to him? Indeed, would I be capable of saying anything, or would the words stick in my throat in such august company? I had no need to worry. The man had no sense of self-importance at all, no airs and graces, not a trace of 'the great I am' about him; he was exactly the person that people saw on their television screens, and from the moment we shook hands it was like being with an old mate, someone I had known for years, someone with whom I was completely comfortable. It remained that way for the many hours I spent in Les's company, at the BBC Television Centre, the rehearsal rooms at North Acton, and at his home in Lytham St Anne's during the six years I spent providing him with some of the words for his shows, words that were improved upon once he had added his perfect inflection, timing and delivery to them before dispensing them to the watching television audience. I have since learned that many comedians are only as funny as the script they have been provided with. Les most certainly wasn't; he was as funny in real life as ever he was on the crystal bucket. (Speaking of my visits to Les's home, on one occasion he had just returned from a family holiday in The Bahamas. Making conversation I asked his wife Meg (Margaret) what she thought of the island. She replied: 'Very nice, but I wouldn't go again.' Cissie & Ada up and dressed, God bless her.)

Les and I had been brought together purely by chance. *The Two Ronnies* producer Peter Whitmore had been handed the task of producing what would be Les's second series since joining the BBC from ITV the year previously. (I recall that a newspaper article claimed that Les had been 'poached' by the BBC. On learning this Les, true to his northern roots, had said: 'I wasn't poached: I was fried, with a generous dollop of brown sauce.' I also remember him adroitly putting down his new employers, saying that the BBC was 'The same as ITV but with O-levels'.)

His first series, *The Les Dawson Show*, hadn't gone down too well and a new vehicle for his talents had been sought. It arrived in the form of an anglicised version of an American show, *Alan King's Final Warning*. King was a master of the elegant rant and employed this talent in the shows by offering amusing and sage advice on coming to terms with modern life and its many pitfalls, his observations further illustrated in short sketches performed by actors. Transplanted to a studio in BBC Television Centre, which for the purposes of the show had been dressed as some sort of futuristic control centre, and decorated with glamorous scantily-clad assistants (whom Les would consistently lust after), *Alan King's Final Warning* became *The Dawson Watch*. What better than Les's pessimist persona to explain the absurdities of the established order of things to the viewing public?

Rather than rely on tried-and-trusted scriptwriters to provide scripts for the show, the BBC, for reasons best known to itself, decided to inflict on Les four writers with very few TV writing credits in their careers thus far: Andy Hamilton, Tom Magee-Engelfield, Colin Bostock-Smith, and me. The following week I was treated to an example of Les's razor-sharp wit when it became apparent that Andy and I were coming up with the sort of material that suited Les whereas, for one reason or another, Tom and Colin weren't. At the script conference prior to show two Peter Whitmore took Les to one side and said: 'Oh by the way, Les, I've had to let Magee-Engelfield and Bostock-Smith go.' Quick as a flash Les replied, 'Well that's got rid of four of the buggers.' On hearing this I feared that he might well

3

have been implying that he now had only to get rid of the two remaining buggers, Andy and myself, and all would be well with the world again. In the event we were kept on, Andy for three series of *The Dawson Watch* before he decided to move on, me for those shows plus the three series of *The Les Dawson Show* that immediately followed them.

I attended all the rehearsals of *The Les Dawson Show*, of which, apart from Les, I was the sole writer. I would write the sketches - Cissie & Ada amongst them - Les would write his stand-up material and we each chipped in with ideas for both. On the first day of rehearsals Les was always word perfect. At first I thought it was because he had taken great pains to learn the script, but the truth is that he had a near photographic memory and had only to read a script once to retain about eighty per cent of it. And the 20 per cent he didn't retain he could always fill in with words of his own invention, words that were quite often funnier than the ones he had failed to remember.

Although Les knew all his lines this wasn't to say that rehearsals were a pleasure. Indeed, until I learned better, they used to scare the hell out of me. The way it went was that Les and his fellow thespians would read through the sketch. Les's performance, with barely a look at the script, would be spot on, all a scriptwriter could hope for. Minutes later, after a few comments and words of advice from the producer, the cast would act out the sketch a second time. This time Les wouldn't be as good. And by the time the participants had rehearsed the sketch a third time Les's performance had diminished in stature from all you could dare hope for, to truly abysmal. Lines that had initially been delivered with panache were now delivered with about as much sparkle as a wet Roman candle; timing that had been perfect was now as out of step as a one-legged soldier. The reason for this, as Les later told me, was that he realised early on in his television acting career that the more he rehearsed a sketch the worse he performed it so that now, after the initial read through, he would simply go through the motions for the rest of the rehearsals in order for it to remain fresh when it really mattered - the performance to the live audience on recording night. Who can argue that his method didn't work perfectly?

I have two abiding memories of Les. The first is the occasion he was standing at the bar of the BBC Club during the hour between dress rehearsal and 'show time' along with Andy, me, and producer Peter Whitmore. Les had already downed a couple of large scotches in short order, during which time Peter hovered anxiously at his elbow, guarding against Les drinking too much. Les ordered a third. Peter frowned. 'Don't you think you've had enough, Les? We've a show to do remember.' Les bade the barman fulfil his order, turned to Peter, and in the voice of a great Shakespeare tragedian actor said: 'I can't go on alone.' Priceless.

The second memory is of another recording night and goes some way to demonstrating the generousness of spirit of Les. With the audience settled in their seats for the 7.30 pm start Les was nowhere to be seen.

Search parties were sent out to all four corners of the Television Centre. The star of the show was eventually run to ground in the BBC canteen telling jokes to two cleaning ladies. The P.A. who found him said: 'Les, for God's sake, there's an audience of three hundred waiting for the show to start.' Les, without showing the slightest concern said, 'Make that three hundred and two,' turned to the cleaning ladies and said, 'Follow me girls.' And they did, to seats in the front row.

CISSIE AND ADA ON TV

The following is what Roy Barraclough had to say about the birth of Cissie & Ada in a TV interview soon after Les's untimely death.

Cissie and Ada was based on the Norman Evans 'Over the Garden Wall' character. The set for these sketches was, literally, a garden wall, and Norman would climb up on a kitchen stool to see over the wall sufficiently, then have a chat with the neighbour next door. Cissie and Ada was a dead pinch from that and no one, especially Les, would deny it, Norman being one of Les's heroes. The difference between Cissie and Ada and Norman was that we were a twosome whereas Norman spoke to an imaginary neighbour who the audience never saw. Norman would say something to the neighbour, 'listen' to the neighbour's imagined answer and so on and so on. Les and I first started doing Cissie and Ada to amuse ourselves at the time we were doing Sez Les for Yorkshire Television and waiting for the technicians to set up the lighting or cameras in the studio. The producer caught us doing it one day and said: "It's not a bad idea for a sketch, we'll do it in the show." At the time we never thought they would go down in comedy history but I'm very proud that they have. We had a lot of fun doing them. It was decided to do a Cissie and Ada sketch every week and after the first one the show's regular scriptwriters - two of them, I remember, were Barry Cryer and David Nobbs - chipped in with bits of the script and eventually took over the responsibility of writing them, with Les and myself adding our bits in rehearsal.

CISSIE & ADA ON STAGE

A THEATRE ADVERTISING NOTICE

Cissie & Ada - An Hysterical Rectomy, featuring Eric Potts (widely known for his portrayal of eccentric baker Diggory Compton in *Coronation Street*) as Ada. Cissie is played by Steve Nallon, known, amongst many other things, for being the voice of Margaret Thatcher in *Spitting Image*, with another *Corrie* favourite, Steven Arnold (Ashley Peacock) playing scriptwriter Terry

Ravenscroft. Written by Graham Warrener and incorporating several Cissie & Ada original sketches from Les Dawson's BBC days, written by Terry Ravenscroft), the show is directed by John-Jackson Almond.

Eric Potts as Ada and Steve Nallon as Cissie

THE CISSIE & ADA ORIGINAL SCRIPTS

On leaving Yorkshire Television for the BBC Les left Cissie & Ada behind him. They appeared neither in the first series of *The Les Dawson Show* nor in the first series of *The Dawson Watch*. Although the first series of *The Dawson Watch* had been quite well received it was thought, both by Andy Hamilton and me, that it would be an even better show if Les were to appear in the sketches, as himself, rather than just fronting the show with actors performing the sketches. It was agreed with Les and the producer that this was the way we were going to go for the second series. With Les now appearing in the sketches I saw this as an ideal opportunity to bring back Cissie & Ada, which I have always felt was a big part of Les Dawson. Happily, especially for me, Les agreed, and Cissie & Ada appeared in all *The Dawson Watch* shows thereafter. And all episodes of the following *The Les Dawson Show* of course.

Writing comedy isn't the easiest of occupations, but writing Cissie & Ada was perhaps easier than most scriptwriting jobs I undertook, principally because as a boy I grew up amongst women much like Cissie, and especially Ada, hair-curlered Ena Sharples-like harridans who would habitually spend part of their day standing on their respective front doorsteps commenting to each other about the disgusting state of the curtains at number 29 over the road - 'She's had them up since D-

Day' - before going on to do a demolition job on the character of the woman at number 14 who was 'No better than she should be' and 'Too friendly with her lodger for my liking - well I heard her bedsprings going at three-o-clock this morning and her husband's on permanent nights.' As a twelve-year-old I remember, on the occasion the horse pulling the Co-op milk cart chose to fill the gutter with pee for about two minutes whilst the milkman was delivering bottles of milk to the door, one woman complaining about this with the words: 'Can't you stop your horse doing that? If I wanted to live next to a canal I'd have moved to Venus.' (It was only later that I found out that she must have meant Venice, but it still made me laugh at the time.)

The following scripts are as written and delivered to Les and the show's producer. They are by and large what were eventually transmitted, although in the process from script to screen most of them have been cut to fit the time slot allowed for them in the show (they almost always went on longer than they should have, very often due to extended laughter caused by Ada's adjusting of her pendulous breasts, and other antics from time to time such as opening her legs and exposing her knickers for all the world to see). And occasionally some of the dialogue was altered for one reason or another, or maybe cut out altogether if it was felt to be a bit too near the knuckle, perhaps a little too rude, for prime time Saturday evening's viewing.

MAKING ECONOMIES

ADA'S KITCHEN. ADA IS BUSY DOING THE IRONING. SHE TAKES A LARGE PAIR OF PINK DIRECTOIRE KNICKERS FROM THE IRONING BASKET, INSPECTS THEM FOR HOLES, LAYS THEM ON THE IRONING BOARD AND COMMENCES TO IRON THEM. THERE IS A TAP ON THE DOOR AND CISSIE COMES IN CARRYING A FRYING PAN.

CISSIE:
Coo-eee, it's only me.

ADA:
(TURNS) Oh it's you Cissie, love. I was just ironing my smalls.

CISSIE:
I was wondering if you could help me out, Chuck, only they've turned my electric off while they're putting my new cooker in. It's Italian you know, to match my Dilusso fitted units. Rather apt when you come to think of it because Leonard and I are heavily into Italian cuisine, Veal Napolitano, that sort of thing. I cook several at once and pop them in the freezer.

ADA:
Fancy.

CISSIE:
Last night we had a frozen risotto.

ADA:
Ours used to do that regular until Bert lagged the pipes.
He made a lovely job of it with the stuffing from an old
duvet and a pair of leg warmers.

CISSIE:
I didn't realise your Bert was into do-it-yourself?

ADA:
Well the council won't do anything, will they. Won't lift
a finger that lot. I'm fed up with complaining about that
hole in our bedroom ceiling, it snowed last night. Me
and Bert woke up in a drift.

CISSIE:
Oh I couldn't be putting up with that sort of thing.

ADA:
It's scandalous, Cissie. Bert spent most of the morning
digging out the jerry. Then he had to grit round the bed
before I got out because you know what I'm like on
snow, with my legs. So you're having a new cooker
fitted, you say? Electric is it?

CISSIE:

Oh yes, I've always sworn by electric. I've always found it more economical.

ADA:

Well it can't be dearer than gas because I just can't keep up with my gas bills. That oven of mine uses more gas than a Zeppelin. You want to see them dials going round on my meter, it looks like the tote on Derby Day. Do you know what my bill was for the last quarter? Seventy-three pounds.

CISSIE:

Yes but then there are appliances on your gas bill, aren't there.

ADA:

No, Bert got his truss on the National Health.

CISSIE:

You see it bumps up you're bill if you're paying for things like gas fires and suchlike. And of course they do make a standing charge.

ADA:

They can make a cavalry charge for all I care, I'm not paying it. I've used nothing like that much gas, I've cut right down. Me and Bert have even took to bathing together to save on hot water.

CISSIE:
Oh I say, that's a bit *risqué*.

ADA:
It's damn risky. It's the last time I let him loose with a loofah I can tell you. My thighs have never been the same since. I make him use a flannel now.

CISSIE:
Well there's nothing wrong with that I suppose, as long as you keep him away from the erogenous zones.

ADA:
Well we're not keen on holidays abroad. Anyway what can I do for you now you're here, Chuck?

CISSIE:
I was wondering if I could use your cooker to finish off this dish I'm making for Leonard's tea. *Coq au vin*. Have you ever tried *coq au vin*?

ADA:
No but I once let an Italian put his hand up my jumper on the back seat of his Fiat.

CISSIE:
Honestly Ada, you really are pig ignorant. *Coq au vin* is French for chicken in wine. And I'd like to finish it off on your cooker if you don't mind.

ADA:

Well you can if you like but I don't think you'll have much joy.

CISSIE:

Well I am used to the convenience of electric of course, but I can work miracles on a gas cooker.

ADA:

You'll need to, they've cut my gas off.

CISSIE:

Oh Ada, love. When did this happen?

ADA:

Yesterday. I was just about to bake a pie for Bert with the rhubarb he's grown in the back garden.

CISSIE:

My Leonard's rhubarb is quite something this year. He puts manure on it.

ADA:

Bert prefers custard on his.

CISSIE:

So how are you managing to cook if they've cut your gas off? I suppose if it came down to it you and Bert could always have a gazpacho.

ADA:

Yes but you can't live on love alone, Cissie, so I thought I'd do kippers.

CISSIE:

And how are you proposing to heat them up?

TWO KIPPERS POP UP OUT OF THE TOASTER.

ADA:

Where there's a will there's a way.

CISSIE:

Well if you want my opinion your mind should be on more important things than feeding your Bert. You should be thinking about how you're going to get yourself out of this financial crisis you've managed to land yourself in.

ADA:

Well don't think I haven't tried to economise, Cissie. I mean I haven't been near a butcher's shop for weeks. The last time we saw red meat in this house was when we were watching the racing on the telly and Lester Piggott used the whip. I've tried everything. I even bake the canary's seeds so they're harder to crack. Do you know something Cissie, I can't even afford a new piece of sandpaper for the bottom of its cage, and you know the state they get in.

17

CISSIE:

Well have you tried to budget?

ADA:

Yes, I've even had a wallpaper scraper on it but there's just no shifting it, it's stuck solid.

CISSIE:

Well we can't have you without gas, that's for sure. (PRODUCES HER PURSE, OPENS IT) So I'll lend you the money. Seventy three pounds wasn't it?

ADA:

Oh I couldn't, Cissie.

CISSIE:

Don't be so daft, what are friends for. You can let me have it back when you're on your feet. Here you are. (HANDS ADA THE MONEY)

ADA:

Bless you, Cissie, whatever would I do without you.

CISSIE:

And mind you keep it away from your Bert. Have you got a safe place to keep it, well away from his clutching hands?

ADA:

Yes. (SHE PICKS UP THE KNICKERS SHE HAS

BEEN IRONING AND PUTS THE MONEY IN THEM)

CISSIE:
You call that a safe place from Bert?

ADA:
It will be when I've put them on.

THE ART GALLERY

AN ART GALLERY. CISSIE & ADA HOVE INTO VIEW. CISSIE IS SHOWING GREAT INTEREST IN THE EXHIBITS, ADA MUCH LESS SO. THEY PAUSE AT A LARGE PAINTING, A LANDSCAPE BY THE FRENCH IMPRESSIONIST CAMILLE PISSARRO. CISSIE IS OBVIOUSLY VERY TAKEN BY THE PAINTING.

CISSIE:
Oh yes. Very artistic, isn't it, Ada.

ADA:
Well if you like trees it is.

CISSIE:
French, if I'm not mistaken. (SHE REFERS TO HER BROCHURE) Yes, I was right. It's a Pissarro.

ADA:
They'll do it anywhere these foreigners.

CISSIE:
Camille Pissarro was a famous Impressionist, Ada.

ADA:
What, you mean like a sort of French Mike Yarwood?

CISSIE:

Honestly Ada, I can't take you anywhere. You're pig ignorant, you really are. Impressionists were a group of painters who painted without elaborate finish or detail.

ADA:

Well the Co-op Decorators do that. You should have seen the state they left my front room skirting boards in, I've seen less streaks on two pounds of belly pork.

CISSIE:

If, as I suspect, you are totally uncomprehending in matters of good taste and breeding, Ada, kindly keep your gob shut!

ADA:

Well there's no need for that, I'm sure.

CISSIE;

Well you'd test the patience of a saint, you really would. I mean you were just the same when I took you to that exhibition of 'Clothing Through the Ages' when we went to Rhyl. Showing me up like that!

ADA:

What do you mean, showing you up?

CISSIE:

You know very well what I mean. When the guide pointed out those corsets and said they were from

William and Mary. And you said 'Are they as good as Marks and Spencers?'

ADA:
Well I'm very sorry I'm sure but some of us haven't had the benefit of your education, have we. I mean I could only go to school every other day, what with being a twin and only one pair of knickers between us.

CISSIE:
But you were both in the school hockey team, surely? What did you do then?

ADA:
If it wasn't my day for the knickers I just prayed it wasn't windy.

CISSIE:
Yes well accompanying me round this art gallery will give you the chance to catch up on your education. It can do you nothing but good.

ADA:
It isn't doing my feet any good, I can tell you that for nothing; they feel like a couple of globe artichokes.

CISSIE:
Oh stop complaining will you, we have a lot to get through yet.

THEY WALK ON. SUDDENLY ADA SEES A STATUE OF A TOTALLY NAKED GREEK GOD. THE SIGHT OF IT STOPS HER IN HER TRACKS.

ADA:
Ooooooh! (SHE QUICKLY COVERS CISSIE'S EYES AND TRIES TO WALK HER PAST THE STATUE)

CISSIE:
What the….what do you think you're playing at, Ada!

ADA:
Just keep walking, Cissie.

CISSIE PUSHES ADA'S HANDS AWAY.

CISSIE:
Get your hands off me, you daft…. (SHE SEES THE STATUE)…oooh! Oh I say.

ADA:
Well I did try to save you from it.

CISSIE:
Yes. Thank you Ada, love, very considerate of you.

NEITHER CISSIE NOR ADA CAN TAKE THEIR EYES OFF THE STATUE'S GENITAL AREA.

ADA:
Disgusting, isn't it.

CISSIE:
Positively scandalous.

THEY BOTH CARRY ON LOOKING AT THE
STATUE, UTTERLY TRANSFIXED.

CISSIE:
I wonder who sculpted it?

ADA:
I don't know, but he wasn't short of clay.

CISSIE:
It could be Moore, I suppose.

ADA:
Oh not much more, surely.

CISSIE:
I meant *Henry* Moore, the sculptor, you soft ha'porth! Or
on second thoughts it could be Rodin. He did 'The
Thinker' you know.

ADA:
Well that would certainly give you something to think
about.

CISSIE:

Honestly Ada, your mind! You've got a point though I must admit, he's certainly a big lad and no mistake.

ADA:

I thought he had three legs at first.

CISSIE:

I wonder what it's called? (SHE NOTICES A PLAQUE AND LEANS FORWARD TO READ IT)

ADA:

Be careful Cissie, it could poke your eye out.

CISSIE:

(READS OFF THE PLAQUE) It's called 'Waiting'.

ADA:

Yes and he'd be waiting a hell of a long time if he was mine. Hey, can you keep a secret, Cissie?

CISSIE:

Well of course I can.

ADA:

That's the first grown-up one I've ever seen.

CISSIE:

Oh come on Ada, you don't expect me to believe that, surely. What about your Bert, you must have seen him undressed?

ADA:

Not once, Cissie. The whole time we've been married.
No, he's always got undressed in the dark. He says it's
because when his mother was carrying him it was during
the war and she was once frightened by a searchlight
operator.

CISSIE:

Well now that you've seen one, what do you think?

ADA:

I think I'm going to go back to the vicar who married us
and ask for a rebate on my marriage licence.

THEY WALK ON.

CHRISTMAS

ADA'S LIVING ROOM. THE AFTERMATH OF A PARTY. CISSIE & ADA, WEARING PARTY HATS, ARE TIDYING UP.

ADA:
That's the trouble with having a Christmas party isn't it Cissie, all the clearing up after.

CISSIE:
What say we take a break then, Chuck?

ADA:
Well just for a few minutes, because I really must find Bert's teeth, he'll be lost without them, the last time he lost them he could only suck rusks until they turned up and there was no living with him.

THEY SIT DOWN ON THE SETTEE.

CISSIE:
Well I must say you did yourself proud tonight Ada, love. Everyone seemed to enjoy themselves at any rate. And the food was excellent, I couldn't fault it.

ADA:
Thank you, Cissie.

CISSIE:

I thought your vol-au-vents really stuck out.

ADA:

Yes it's this new bra. It both lifts and separates - after a bit of a struggle.

CISSIE:

It's marvellous what technology can do nowadays, isn't it. You know they do say that the modern bra is based on the cantilever.

ADA:

I could have done with a tyre lever.

CISSIE:

(LOOKS AROUND HER) I don't suppose there's any drink left?

ADA:

Only that home-made sherry that Bert made last week.

CISSIE:

Ah, the golden nectar of old Jerez.

ADA:

No he brewed it in a bucket. Would you like a drop?

CISSIE:

Well I wouldn't say no because I've always been partial

to a drop of sherry. Such a refined drink I've always thought. Yet at the same time there's something about it that gives it an almost aphrodisiac quality.

ADA:
Yes, it gives me the wind too. (SHE GETS THE BOTTLE OF SHERRY) You're lucky, it's nearly empty. It's a wonder there's any left at all what with Bert's relatives. Did you see the drunken louts; they'll drink anything that's in a bottle, one of them finished up on double body deodorants.

CISSIE:
Yes, from what I saw of them their manners left much to be desired.

ADA:
I was ashamed, Cissie. Ashamed. Did you see them round my running buffet? They were like a shoal of piranha fish. Anybody would think they'd never seen food before. And did you see his cousin Mavis going at my home-made mutton pate? She scraped half the willow pattern off the plate, I've got two Japanese lovers stood in mid-air and no bridge.

CISSIE:
Wasn't her first husband that nice Higgins lad?

ADA:
Arthur.

29

CISSIE:

That's him. Too good for her, I'm sure. I can't think what he ever saw in her.

ADA:

Bert says he only married her because he's a fisherman and he thought she had worms. Shameless hussy she is. I mean I wouldn't have minded if she'd kept her children in check but she just lets them run riot. I could have strangled that little Jason of hers. Did you see what he was trying to do to our cat with that young doctor's outfit?

CISSIE:

I hope the young rapscallion didn't harm it.

ADA:

I wouldn't know, it's still on the roof with its legs crossed. I mean they've no right giving children presents like that, no right at all.

CISSIE:

My word it isn't like it was in our day, is it. All I ever got in my Christmas stocking was a whip and top and an orange.

ADA:
And glad of it.

CISSIE:

And our Ralph, even when he was in long trousers he only had a little dinky.

ADA:

Well they can't all be on the front row when they're handed out.

CISSIE:

Even so he used to get hours of enjoyment playing with it up in his bedroom.

ADA:

Well what man doesn't?

CISSIE:

Yes he played with it so much that eventually all the paint chipped off it through it banging against the skirting boards.

ADA:

What?

CISSIE:

And speaking of Christmas presents what did you get for your Bert this year?

ADA:

Well he asked me for something useful so I got him a bottle-opener.

CISSIE:

Well that should certainly be useful; I've never known a man drink so much as your Bert.

ADA:

Cissie there's that many beer bottles in our backyard the estate agent says it's put two hundred pounds on the value of the property.

CISSIE:

I can believe it. And what did he get for you?

ADA:

Well I asked him for a pair of leg warmers. Because you know how I suffer with my legs in the cold weather. I just can't seem to keep them warm. They've been the same ever since I had that affair with that assistant manager from Iceland. You wouldn't believe how I suffer, and I've tried everything. The only thing that worked was when I lagged them with two black dustbin bags, but it got Bert too excited. That reminds me, I haven't found his teeth yet.

CISSIE:

Well when did he last have them?

ADA:

He had them in bed last night, definitely, because I'd just settled under the duvet with the hot water bottle on my rheumatism when he snuggled right up to me, kissed me on the back of the neck and began to bite me.

CISSIE:
Bite you?

ADA:
All over, Cissie.

CISSIE:
Oh I say! How erotic. And did you respond?

ADA:
Well you know me Cissie, I can take it or leave it. Nowadays I'd just as soon cuddle up with a Mills and Boon to tell you the truth. But suddenly....I began to feel hot all over.

CISSIE:
He'd awaken your desires, had he?

ADA:
No he'd bitten through the hot water bottle.

HOLIDAYS

A TRAVEL AGENCY. CISSIE & ADA WALK IN. CISSIE NOTICES THERE IS NOBODY AT THE COUNTER.

CISSIE:
There doesn't appear to be anyone here, Ada love.

ADA:
Perhaps they've gone on their holidays.

THEY SIT DOWN TO WAIT.

CISSIE:
While we're waiting it will give us the chance to decide where we want to go this year.

ADA:
Well anywhere as long as it isn't Greece, I didn't like that Rhodes place last year.

CISSIE:
I told you, you should have gone to Athens, you'd have liked it there, it's lovely, they have an Acropolis.

ADA:

They had one in Rhodes too, I was never off it.

CISSIE:

Oh you really are coarse at times, Ada. Not to mention uneducated. The Acropolis is an old ruin!

ADA:

So was this, it had a crack in it and a loose board.

CISSIE:

Well forget all about that and think of somewhere we can go to. I quite fancy Italy, myself.

ADA:

Me too, a coach tour would be nice.

CISSIE:

How about the Dolomites?

ADA:

Well if they start to play me up I can always sit on an inflatable rubber ring. I quite fancy Blackpool too, to tell you the truth.

CISSIE:

Oh I find it so uncouth, Blackpool.

ADA:

Yes, nice isn't it. Me and Bert had our honeymoon there,

you know. It's the place where I finally became a woman - that first night at the Seaview guest house.

CISSIE:
And tell me Ada - girl talk here - when you went on your honeymoon, were you *virgo intacta*?

ADA:
No, just bed and breakfast.

CISSIE:
I mean that prior to your honeymoon you and Bert hadn't done it?

ADA:
Cissie! I've never heard such mucky talk from you. Muck mucky muck muck.

CISSIE:
Nonsense Ada, it's only human nature.

ADA:
I suppose so. Can you keep a secret, Cissie? Bert didn't know how to do it.

CISSIE:
Really? I must say I find that very hard to believe, knowing your Bert as I do.

ADA:

May God strike me dead, Cissie. He hadn't got a clue. My mother told me to lie back and think of England. I'd time to think of England, Scotland, Ireland, Algeria.....

CISSIE:

Oh you poor dear.

ADA:

And I did everything in my power to tempt him, everything in my power Cissie.

CISSIE:

Did you wear a sexy night-gown?

ADA:

Yes, it was the one I got from Silky Billy's stall on the market, off the bargain rail, two and threepence.

CISSIE:

Was it see-through?

ADA:

Oh yes. Yes you could see my vest and liberty bodice through it as plain as day. Anyway I went to the doctor to see if he could suggest anything and he told me to try taking Bert past the Tower a few times.

CISSIE:

Auto suggestion.

ADA:

No we drove past in a landau. And I walked him past it several times too.

CISSIE:

And did he....you know....rise to the occasion, as it were?

ADA:

Well I'll put it this way; I think he must have been looking at the Central Pier, not the tower.

CISSIE:

Well I don't know about us going to Blackpool for our holiday I would have thought you would want to steer well clear of the place after an experience like that.

ADA:

That's why I want to go; I'm hoping he'll leave me alone again.

CISSIE:

And where does Bert want to go?

ADA:

Well he did once mention that he'd always wanted to return to the place where he spent the war.

CISSIE:

What, the glasshouse at Colchester?

ADA:

No, I mean before he stole that tank. Normandy.

CISSIE:

Now that's not such a bad idea, because my Leonard would like that. He saw action at Normandy, you know. That was where he almost got the VC.

ADA:

Well that's the chance you take when you go with foreign women. The hussies!

CISSIE:

I think we'll settle for Normandy then. Now how shall we travel there, on the cross-channel ferry or shall we fly?

ADA:

Oh the ferry, because it cost us an extra thirty quid the only time me and Bert ever flew.

CISSIE:

Thirty pounds? Why was that?

ADA:

Well you know that little paper bag they give you?

CISSIE:

Yes.

ADA:

Well Bert asked the stewardess what it was for. And she told him it was to be sick in.

CISSIE:

So why did that cost you another thirty pounds?

ADA:

Well he had to drink three bottles of whisky before he felt sick.

SÉANCE

ADA'S LIVING ROOM. CISSIE & ADA ARE SEATED AT A TABLE. ADA IS LOOKING MORE THAN A LITTLE APPREHENSIVE ABOUT THE SITUATION WHILST CISSIE IS MUCH MORE COMFORTABLE WITH IT.

CISSIE:
So it's your mother you'd like to contact then, is it Ada?

ADA:
Yes, if that witch friend of yours ever gets here. She said she'd be here for eight.

CISSIE:
Well it's only just turned. And Mrs Scattergood isn't a witch, she's a medium, she has occult powers. You ought to think yourself lucky she's agreed to do a séance for you because mediums like Mrs Scattergood are few and far between.

ADA:
Sort of medium rare, is she? (LAUGHS. CISSIE GIVES HER A REPROVING LOOK) Sorry Cissie love, it's just that I'm a bit nervous about it all.

CISSIE:

Well that is understandable I suppose. After all this will be the first time you've ever tried to contact the dead, won't it.

ADA:

Apart from when I try to get Bert up for work. Tell me Chuck, when you contact the dead....do you hear their voice?

CISSIE:

No. No the communication from the astral body comes through the medium, Mrs Scattergood.

ADA:

Fancy that. How?

CISSIE:

Well mostly through her Ouija.

ADA:

Through her wee jar? Well we have a jerry for that but to each his own.

CISSIE:

Not her *wee jar*, her *Ouija*. You know. (SHE POINTS AT ADA'S CROTCH) She talks through it.

ADA: (CROSSES HER LEGS AT THE THOUGHT)
Oh I don't like the sound of that , Cissie. Isn't it painful?

CISSIE:

Well she does pull a face sometimes. Then she goes into a trance.

ADA:

I'm not surprised, I'd be in more than a trance if an astral body started talking through my Ouija.

CISSIE:

But sometimes she doesn't bother with the Ouija method at all and simply calls up the spirits by asking them if there's anybody there. That's usually followed by an eerie silence.

ADA:

I have the same trouble when I ring the gas board to complain about my pressure. And what else can she do, this Mrs Scattergood woman?

CISSIE:

Well I believe she's quite expert at levitation.

ADA:

We always get the plumber in when ours is blocked. But if she's reasonable and handy with a plunger I'll try her the next time it happens, what's her number?

CISSIE:

Honestly Ada, you are so uneducated. Don't you know anything about mind over matter?

ADA:

No but Bert does. He uses it to control our sex life.

CISSIE:

Control your sex life? How do you mean?

ADA:

If he's in the mind, my feelings don't matter. It's true Cissie, he doesn't give a damn about how I feel about it. He comes home from that pub at chucking out time and there's no stopping him. It's like trying to hang onto a beer barrel with legs. Every night's the same with him. You want to see my side of the bed, there's no nap left on my flannelette sheets.

CISSIE:

Perhaps you should try separate beds?

ADA:

No fear, he might use his as a springboard. I mean I wouldn't mind Cissie but sometimes he hasn't even got the decency to wake me up, there's many the time I've woken up halfway through.

CISSIE:

Yes well that is of course the advantage of being married to a gentleman like my Leonard. You see if I don't feel in the mood Leonard respects my feelings and exercises control over his libido.

ADA:

Yes but we haven't got a dog now since it ran off. And Bert wouldn't take it for a walk even if we had one, the laggard.

CISSIE:

No, you misunderstand me, Chuck. Your libido is your sexual drive. The ideal situation is when your partner's needs and your needs are in tandem.

ADA:

Well if he thinks he's doing it to me on a bike he's got another think coming. Not one with a pump anyway, God knows what he'd do with that.

CISSIE:

Well perhaps your mother can give you some advice if Mrs Scattergood manages to contact her, because if anybody knew how to handle a man your mother did.

ADA:

She did that, Cissie. I remember her once taking my father's Sunday dinner to the pub, roast brisket and mash and two veg with bread pudding for afters. He was so surprised he missed the double twenty.

CISSIE:
And what did he do?

ADA:

He went for the bull.

CISSIE:

Anyway you still haven't told me why you want to contact your mother?

ADA:

Well it's to do with when she went Cissie, when she passed over.

CISSIE:

When she joined the choir invisible.

ADA:

No she was never in the Salvation Army. I'll never forget her going, Cissie. She lay there on her deathbed and I'd just put the best sheets on because the doctor was coming and she said to me: 'Ada, I've never asked for much, but with the insurance money I'd like you to get a nice stone.'

CISSIE:

And did you?

ADA:

(POLISHES THE STONE IN HER RING) Yes and I've worn it ever since, in her memory, ever since she took her last ride. It was Bert who took her, you know, on her last ride.

CISSIE:
Bert? I didn't know Bert ever drove a hearse.

ADA:
No, we couldn't afford a hearse but he'd just got this job as a milkman with Express Dairies so he took her on his float. It took us four hours to get to the church.

CISSIE:
Four hours? But it's only about a mile away from your house.

ADA:
I know but he had to keep stopping to deliver the milk.

CISSIE:
I believe she took her last breath under mysterious circumstances, didn't she? Wasn't she asphyxiated?

ADA:
No we had he buried.

CISSIE:
I mean that she choked.

ADA:
Yes, on a slice of her home-made Bakewell tart. I'll never forgive myself, Cissie.

CISSIE:

You mustn't blame yourself, it wasn't you fault, Ada.

ADA:

It was, Cissie. Me and Bert had gone to her house for tea. And there was this one piece of Bakewell tart left, and you know what a lovely Bakewell tart my mother made, so naturally both me and Bert had our eyes on it. But I insisted my mother had it and it must have gone down the wrong pipe....she turned black Cissie, I can see her now, Frank Bruno isn't that black....then she went, just like that.

CISSIE:

Yes I can see now why you want to contact her. So you can apologise to her for insisting she had the last piece of Bakewell tart.

ADA:

No, I want her to give me the recipe.

AT THE DOCTOR'S

A DOCTOR'S WAITING ROOM. CISSIE IS WAITING HER TURN. ADA COMES IN. CISSIE IS PLEASED OF THE COMPANY.

CISSIE:
Oh Hello Ada love, sit yourself down next to me. What brings you to the Doctor's?

ADA:
I keep having these funny turns Cissie, these dizzy do's.

CISSIE:
Oh I don't like the sound of that at all.

ADA:
And I keep getting these hot flushes.

CISSIE:
Oh I say! What do you think might be causing them?

ADA:
Well I am at a funny age, Cissie. I mean I am approaching the change.

CISSIE:
You? Approaching the change?

ADA:
Yes.

CISSIE:
From which direction?

ADA:
What do you mean?

CISSIE:
Well I thought your battery would have run down years ago.

ADA:
Oh no. No, my family has always retained its child-bearing years a lot longer than most. Yes, we've always been very fertile. Our Bertha fell pregnant when she was fifty-nine and she swears she only walked past a sausage factory. Anyway to be on the safe side I thought it would be best if the doctor gave me a check-up, what with Bert rediscovering his sex drive.

CISSIE:
Bert's rediscovered his sex drive then?

ADA:
I've a job to keep up with him if the truth be told, Cissie. We'd have gone right through the bedroom wall last night if I hadn't taken the castors off the bed. He was like an animal.

50

CISSIE:

I wonder what's brought that on?

ADA:

Well I did mention it to the doctor the last time I was here and he seems to think it's the side effects from the hormones in the pills he gave Bert for his gout.

CISSIE:

So it appears that as long as Bert is taking those pills for his gout he'll carry on in the same way then?

ADA:

It looks like it, yes.

CISSIE:

Oh you poor dear. And what are you doing about it?

ADA:

Stamping on his foot, regular.

CISSIE:

Well let's just hope you don't fall pregnant again my girl, you won't be wanting another at your time of life, I mean you're not getting any younger.

ADA:

God forbid, Cissie. I mean I went though agony with my last, our Ernest, through agony. You want to see my stretch marks, when I'm stripped off I look like sixteen stones of Danish blue. I carried him for eleven months you know.

CISSIE:
Well there is one thing to be said in favour of carrying over your time, you do tend to give birth more quickly.

ADA:
I didn't, I was in labour longer than Atlee. And I didn't have a normal birth when it finally came, either.

CISSIE:
You didn't have a Caesarean did you?

ADA:
No but I was once very friendly with a Spaniard. Pedro, he was called. Nice lad from Barcelona.

CISSIE:
So it sounds like you had complications giving birth to your Ernest?

ADA:
I'll say. One of them was that they put me in the wrong ward when I got there; they put me in the ward where they treated disorders of the bowels.

CISSIE:
Well I assume that you soon told them you should have been in the maternity ward.

ADA:

Yes but not before they'd given me an enema.

CISSIE:

So when did you go?

ADA:

About two minutes after they'd given it me. And I only just made it to the lavvy in time. Thank God there wasn't a queue.

CISSIE:

I mean when did you go to the *maternity* ward?

ADA:

The following day. That was worse if anything. I can't begin to tell you what I went through in that maternity ward Cissie, terrible it was, I had more gas and air than a barrage balloon. And the midwife was hopeless, I was in labour for thirty six hours before she realised I still had my tights on.

CISSIE:

Oh you poor dear.

ADA:

Then finally my water broke. One of the nurses said she hadn't seen anything like it since she saw *The Dam Busters* at the pictures.

CISSIE:

Still it was all worth it wasn't it, because when it was finally all over you had a lovely baby boy to show for it.

ADA:

Ten pounds, four ounces and five stitches. I'm very small made you know.

CISSIE:

Me too, I had six stitches with my youngest. I suppose Bert came to visit you, after the birth?

ADA:

Yes. When he held the baby he said it had a cleft chin.

CISSIE:

Your Ernest hasn't got a cleft chin.

ADA:

I know, Bert had him upside down.

CISSIE:

The wastrel would be drunk I suppose, from wetting the baby's head.

ADA:

No, when he came he didn't even know I'd had a baby.

CISSIE:

It would be quite a surprise for him then.

ADA:

It was, he thought I'd only gone in hospital to have my appendicts out.

PRISON VISITORS

CISSIE & ADA ARE IN A BARE ANTE-ROOM WAITING TO VISIT ADA'S HUSBAND BERT, WHO IS DOING TIME IN PRISON. CISSIE TAKES IN HER SURROUNDINGS AND SNIFFS WITH DISAPPROVAL.

CISSIE:
So this is what the inside of a prison looks like, I've always wondered.

ADA:
Well thanks to my Bert you know now.

CISSIE:
(LOOKS AROUND HER AND SNIFFS WITH DISTASTE) Strangeways.

ADA:
Yes, Bert has very strange ways. You won't believe some of the things he's tried to make me do in that bed, Cissie.

CISSIE:
Utterly depressing in here isn't it. However four walls do not a prison make.

ADA:

Four walls made a prison for me when the knob came off our lavatory door. I shouted myself hoarse. You should have seen my tonsils, they looked like I'd been gargling with the Harpic. By the way Cissie, thanks for coming with me, to visit Bert.

CISSIE:

Against my better judgement I can assure you, my lady. I shudder to think what my Leonard would think if he knew where I was. He thinks I've gone to Debenhams pricing something for the bathroom. I'm toying with the idea of a new WC.

ADA:

Perhaps Bert will let you use his bucket.

CISSIE:

Tell me, how is the reprobate coping with being incarcerated?

ADA:

Well you can hardly tell he is incarcerated except for a slight limp.

CISSIE:

I hope he isn't getting too depressed.

ADA:

No I think he's quite taken to it actually. I believe he's

very friendly with the Prison Governor.

CISSIE:
What gives you that idea?

ADA:
Well they've given him his own cell, in solitary.

CISSIE:
They've put him in solitary because he'll have been been misbehaving himself, you fool! They'll have put him on bread and water.

ADA:
It'll be a home from home for him then.

CISSIE:
Well at least when you see him you'll be able to bring him succour.

ADA:
Yes I've bought him a bag of Mint Imperials. And some stomach medicine, I thought I'd better.

CISSIE:
Stomach medicine?

ADA:
Yes, when he wrote to me he said he was having a lot of trouble with the screws. And he asked me to bring him a

cake with a hacksaw in it as well.

CISSIE:
Ada you haven't....!

ADA:
Yes, I bought this. (SHE DIPS IN HER SHOPPING BAG AND PRODUCES A FOOT LONG SPONGE CAKE WITH A HACKSAW HANDLE STICKING OUT OF ONE END)

CISSIE:
Well I can't see you getting that past the guards with that, it's quite obvious what it is!

ADA:
Yes you're right, and it would be a shame to let them abdicate it, wouldn't it. (SHE BREAKS OFF A PIECE OF THE CAKE AND HANDS IT TO CISSIE) Here, try a piece, it's Mary Baker Vienna sponge. There's three eggs in that.

CISSIE: (TAKES A BITE)
Hmm, very tasty. Tell me, Ada, you never gave me the whole story, but how exactly did Bert manage to land himself in this fix?

ADA:
Pure bad luck, Cissie. I mean I know Bert's a bit of a tearaway but he's mostly managed to keep himself on

59

the right side of the law. What happened was just a momentary lapse.

CISSIE:
Why what did he do?

ADA:
Stole seventeen cars. He was picked out in an identity parade. I think the starting handle gave him away.

CISSIE:
Ada in no way can stealing seventeen cars be described as a momentary lapse. But tell me about the details of the court case, judicial proceedings have always been an interest of mine what with Leonard being a J.P.

ADA:
You don't say.

CISSIE:
Oh yes, we never miss *Crown Court* on the telly. And we're both fond of Rumpole of course.

ADA:
I know, I've heard your bedsprings going.

CISSIE:
I assume that before Bert appeared he asked for legal aid?

ADA:

No, he had a pint of lager. He said he needed it before he faced the judge. But you should have seen him in that dock, Cissie. He was magnificent. He stood there, gripping the mahogany rail, drew himself up to his full height and positively thundered at the judge: 'I am innocent m'lud, and furthermore I do not recognise this court'. The judge said: 'Why not?' Bert said: 'You've had it decorated since I was last here'.

CISSIE:

I bet that caused some amusement in the Assizes. I say I bet a titter ran round the court when he said that.

ADA:

No, there wasn't anyone from the corset shop in sight.

CISSIE:

So what happened then?

ADA:

Well Bert re-stated his innocence and asked for twelve other cases to be taken into consideration. Then he made an impassioned plea for clemency and the judge gave him six months. Bert was ever so grateful. He went down on his bended knees and said: 'Thank you Your Worship, bless you for being so lenient with me'. And the judge said: 'Not at all, if you'd kept your trap shut I was going to let you off'.

AT THE SEASIDE

THE BEACH. CISSIE & ADA ARE RELAXING IN DECKCHAIRS, SHOES OFF, DRESSES TUCKED INTO THEIR KNICKERS. CISSIE IS RUBBING IN SUN OIL.

CISSIE:
A good idea of yours this, Ada, a week at the seaside away from our menfolk. It'll be a nice break for us. I mean we've only been here a couple of hours and already I'm in the mood to let myself go.

ADA:
I think I'll have to loosen my corsets, too.

CISSIE:
(NOTICES SOMETHING NEARBY) Oh look, Ada, there's the donkeys see.

ADA:
Hey, shall we have a go on one, Cissie?

CISSIE:
No we shall not have a go on one! Perish the thought. I remember the last time you went on a donkey. You rode it right into the sea!

ADA:

I took a sudden fancy to a paddle.

CISSIE:

On a donkey?

ADA:

Well I thought it would be all right, what with it being called Nelson.

CISSIE:

Well it wasn't all right, was it. When the tide came in and trapped you on that sandbank. I could have died when you took your knickers off and started waving them about.

ADA:

Well I wanted to attract somebody's attention.

CISSIE:

You certainly did that. Especially when the breeze got up.

ADA:

What? You don't mean....? God love us, Cissie, you couldn't see my.....could you?

CISSIE:

Well of course you could you fool, why do you think all those men were cheering?

64

ADA:

Fancy that. (SMILES) Men cheering at me showing my fairy. (SHE GETS UP)

CISSIE:

Where are you going?

ADA:

For another donkey ride.

CISSIE:

Oh no you are not lady, sit down!

ADA:

Well perhaps I better hadn't, because I'm trying to forget all about Bert and donkeys always remind me of him.

CISSIE:

They remind you of Bert?

ADA:

When he's going to work.

CISSIE:

Oh, you mean the slow reluctant plod with the head hanging down.

ADA:

No I mean he walks for fifty yards then turns back.

CISSIE:

Incidentally, how will he manage on his own, your Bert? I mean he can't cook can he.

ADA:

The world's worst. He could burn water, that one. So I've left him a big pan of ash with two big tins of Fray Bentos corned beef in it. He'll eat that. Well he will once he realises there's nothing else for him. And if he doesn't like it he can lump it. Or he can eat some of the vegetables he's growing in the back garden.

CISSIE:

I didn't realise Bert had started growing vegetables?

ADA:

Oh yes, he's grown some lovely tomatoes.

CISSIE:

Does he have growbags?

ADA:

Only since his hernia. Well you need something roomy when you're wearing a truss.

CISSIE:

There's one thing for certain, my Leonard will be well catered for while he's on his own.

ADA:

Oh?

CISSIE:

No matter what his gastronomic desires, we have it in the freezer.

ADA:

Well whatever turns you on, but don't the baskets leave marks on your bottom?

CISSIE:

Ada you really are coarse. You've got a mind like a cesspool, you really have.

ADA:

Well I can't help it if you're narrow-minded.

CISSIE:

Me? Narrow-minded?

ADA:

Well you are. You always have been, you've put up with chicken drumsticks for years because you don't like asking for breast. You've always been the same, ever since.....(SHE SEES SOMETHING IN THE FAR DISTANCE)...ooooh!

CISSIE:

What's the matter?

ADA:

(POINTS) That girl there! Naked as the day she was born. Look at her prancing about, the young hussy!

CISSIE:

Now who's being narrow-minded.

ADA:

Well there's a time and a place for everything.

CISSIE:

But this is the time and the place Ada, they allow nude sunbathing on this beach, didn't you know?

ADA:

Never!

CISSIE:

Oh yes, they're quite permissive here now. Two years ago you had to wear a bikini at the very least. Last year you could go topless. And this year you're allowed to be totally naked.

ADA GETS UP AND STARTS PACKING UP.

CISSIE:

What are you doing?

ADA:

I'm clearing off before they make it compulsory.

AWAY DAY

A RAILWAY CARRIAGE. CISSIE IS SEATED, READING A WOMENS' GLOSSY MAGAZINE. ADA COMES DOWN THE GANGWAY CARRYING TWO PACKETS OF SANDWICHES AND CARTONS OF COFFEE. SHE SITS DOWN NEXT TO CISSIE.

CISSIE:
You took your time, what kept you?

ADA:
I bumped into May Scattergood and her fancy man.

CISSIE:
Yes well that one's only as good as she should be.

ADA:
Just.

CISSIE:
So they're on an away day to London too, are they?

ADA:
More like an have it away day if I know May.

CISSIE:
Yes, and her husband dead for less than a month.

ADA: I went to the funeral. She couldn't get him in the ground fast enough. It's the first time I've ever seen a coffin arrive in an E-type Jaguar. (HANDS CISSIE A PACKET OF SANDWICHES) Here you are, there was a queue at the buffet and they'd nearly run out of everything so I couldn't get you what you asked for.

CISSIE:
Did you take pot luck?

ADA:
No it was engaged, there was a queue for that as well.

CISSIE:
And they say this is the age of the train.

ADA:
This one must be about ninety three.

CISSIE:
That Jimmy Savile has a lot to answer for, hasn't he. What's that thing he said on that TV commercial - 'Let the train take the strain'?

ADA:
It's not the only thing that's taking the strain, these new corsets I got from Madame Hetty's are killing me. I

think I'll take them off in the superloo before we go to the theatre.

CISSIE:
Ah, the theatre! I'm really looking forward to tonight.

ADA:
Me too. It'll bring back memories, because I was an actress myself once, you know.

CISSIE:
You?

ADA:
Oh yes, when I was a girl, I was with the Collyhurst Strolling Players.

CISSIE:
I didn't know you'd had experience on the boards.

ADA:
Yes. but only once because I got splinters in my bottom and Bert complained it made his knees sore.

CISSIE:
(REMEMBERS) That's if we can get tickets for the theatre! I mean thanks to you we haven't got any. I don't know why I ever agreed to let you send off for them after what happened the last time.

ADA:

What do you mean?

CISSIE:

When you sent off for tickets for *Les Miserables* and we ended up with two seats for the *Festival of Erotica*.

ADA:

Well I thought it would be like the Festival of Britain. You know, with a Dome of Discovery.

CISSIE:

Well I discovered a few things I can tell you!

ADA:

And me. I'd never seen an ostrich in black leather and suspenders before.

CISSIE:

Then against my better judgement I agreed to let you send off for tickets again. I still don't believe what you did. I mean you actually had the tickets in your hands, Ada. Two tickets for my favourite musical, *The Sound of Music*. Two of the very best seats in the orchestra stalls. And you sent them back with a note saying 'If I'm paying ten pounds for a ticket I'm damned if I'm sitting with the band'.

ADA:

Anybody can make a mistake, Cissie.

CISSIE:

So now we shall have to try to get tickets for something else, because that's fully booked now. I wouldn't mind seeing *Cats* myself, what do you think?

ADA:

No thank you, I see enough of cats at home. I could choke that one next door. You want to see the way it's affected the soil in Bert's potato patch. It's took all the chrome off his fork.

CISSIE:

Are you sure it isn't that new kitten of yours that's to blame?

ADA:

No, our kitten's no trouble at all. Now it's stopped leaving messages on the lino.

CISSIE:

You see you wouldn't have any trouble with cats at all if you kept a dog, like Leonard and I.

ADA:

Oh yes, you've got a pooch now haven't you.

CISSIE:

Prince is hardly a pooch, Ada. He's a pedigree Afghan hound. Actually we've got big hopes for him, there's already some other Afghan owners have requested his services as a stud.

ADA:
Fancy.

CISSIE:
And Leonard and I are thinking of showing him.

ADA:
Why, doesn't it know how to do it? I'll stand by with a bucket of water.

CISSIE:
Really Ada, you are the limit! You've got sex on the brain.

ADA:
Oh I wouldn't say that.

CISSIE:
Well I would! You think of nothing else. I remember when you filled in your passport application form. Against 'Sex' you put 'Once a night and twice on Sundays'.

ADA:
Well I'm not one to show off.

CISSIE:
I don't know why I associate with you, I really don't,

much less accompany you to the London theatre. Particularly after that episode when we went to the ballet at Sadler's Wells.

ADA:
Oh it was beautiful, *Swan Lake*, wasn't it.

CISSIE:
Well I don't know how you'd know that I'm sure, you spent the entire evening gazing at the bulge in the leading man's tights.

ADA:
Well you must admit it he was a well endowed lad.

CISSIE:
For your information Ada what you were so enthralled by was his codpiece.

ADA:
His what?

CISSIE:
It was his codpiece.

ADA:
Well if it was it was the biggest fish finger I've ever clapped eyes on.

WAITRESSES

CISSIE AND ADA HAVE TAKEN ON PART-TIME JOBS IN A LOCAL FRENCH RESTAURANT TO BRING A LITTLE MORE MONEY IN. WE DISCOVER THEM SNEAKING FIVE MINUTES TO THEMSELVES.

ADA:
(SIGHS) Oh I say, Cissie, it's a relief to take the weight off your feet isn't it. (SHE TAKES ONE OF HER SHOES OFF, LOOKS AT THE SOLE AND PULLS A FACE) Ugh. I'll kill that cat. (SHE PUTS BOTH SHOES IN A NEARBY ICE BUCKET TO COOL OFF. STEAM FROM THE ICE BUCKET EMERGES) Just look at my feet, Cissie. I've got toes like Bert's crocus bulbs. It's all that rushing about.

CISSIE:
Well it's your own fault, isn't it. You should wear sensible shoes. They warned you about that at the Manpower Services.

ADA:
I know, love, but I have very awkward feet.

CISSIE:
They're not on their own.

ADA:

I can either wear traditional courts, French sabots or pumps. I went to one of those chirrupodopolists About them. (SHE PRODUCES A MINI BOTTLLE OF BRANDY FROM HER HAT AND TAKES A SWIG, MUCH TO CISSIE'S SURPRISE GREAT AND DISAPPROVAL) He took one look at my feet and he went quite pale. He said I've got rancid bunions and they'll have to come off before gangrene sets in.

CISSIE: (ALARMED) Hey. Look out, here comes Monsieur Jacques. Look busy. (SHE PICKS UP A SPOON AN STARTS POLISHING IT WITH HER APRON)

ADA:

Monsieur Jacques! Don't talk rubbish. You know who it is, don't you? It's Arnold Birchenhough from number twelve down on Westbold Street. The house with the purple tulles and the hamster in the window.

CISSIE:

The one who married Elsie Farnsbarns, runs the pick 'n mix counter at Pricejoys?

ADA:

That's the one. Well she's had six kids before, you know.

CISSIE:

I didn't know that!

ADA:

To an Algerian in Folkestone. She was in charge of an ack ack battery. Yes, apparently they....performed....while there was a lull in the bombing. He told her he was a Polish count. He came from Bootle.

CISSIE:

So it was a marriage of convenience, you might say.

ADA:

No, they got married in church. She'd no right to, you know. She got married in white. She drifted down the aisle like an Alp. Well he'd certainly been up her, that's for sure.

CISSIE:

She must have looked like an avalanche.

ADA:

It was a good job the vicar was a midwife. I'll tell you something else as well, Chuck. The baby was born with a broken arm.

CISSIE:

What caused that do you think?

ADA:
It was trying to hang on until after the wedding.

CISSIE:
(LOOKS AROUND) There aren't many customers in tonight, are there. It's very quiet.

ADA:
It's Monsieur Henri's cooking. It's muck.

CISSIE:
Muck?

ADA:
Muck. Muck muck muck muck muck.

CISSIE:
Oh I can't agree with you there, Chuck. He's quite adventurous is Monsieur Henri.

ADA:
You've no need to tell me that, I can't go in that kitchen without him trying to put his hand up my skirt.

CISSIE:
I mean his cooking.. There's snails on the menu tonight.

ADA:
Well that doesn't surprise me at all, he never washes the cabbage.

CISSIE:

You fool, I was referring to the edible snails. L'Escargot.

ADA:

He's no damn right selling horse meat if you ask me.

CISSIE:

What are you talking about, he doesn't sell horsemeat?

ADA:

What? You just said he did.

CISSIE:

I never did.

ADA:

Yes you did. You said Les Escargot. Well I backed that in the Grand National. I had it in the Labour Club sweep and backed it fifty pee each way. I could have saved myself fifty pee there because they only went one way. You can mark my words, Cissie, that grilled sirloin will have whipping marks on it the way that jockey was leathering it. (SHE LIFTS UP HER DRESS A LITTLE AND PRODUCES ANOTHER MINI BOTTLE OF BRANDY FROM THE LEG OF HER KNICKERS. UNCORKS IT AND TAKES A SWIG)

CISSIE:

(DISGUSTED) Well I don't know where that came from but I know where it's going. You trouble is you're uncouth, Ada, absolutely uncouth. There too much of this drink drink drink all the time with you. I've warned you before - when the wine is in the wit is out. I mean Monsieur Henri's culinary expertise is known the length and breadth of Bacup. It's second to none, *par excellence*. You should see what that man can do *a la carte*.

ADA:
I've seen what he can do in the back of his Mini, that's enough for me.

DINER
Ladies! Service please!

CISSIE:
Oh, that man's is a little trier, isn't he.

ADA:
I don't know what's wrong got into him, he's only been waiting an hour.

CISSIE:
Oh he's always awkward, He comes in often. He always goes for the *piece de resistance*.

ADA:
He's probably got a weak bladder.

CISSIE:
Honestly, Ada. *Must* you be so coarse.

ADA ACCIDENTALLY PUTS HER HAND IN A LARGE GATEAU ON THE ADJACENT SWEETS TROLLEY. SHE LICKS CREAM OFF HER HAND WITH GREAT ENJOYMENT, MUCH TO CISSIE'S DISGUST.

ADA:
Waste not, want not.

ADA ENJOYS THE GATEAU SO MUCH SHE SAMPLES ANOTHER OFF THE TROLLEY. THIS ONE CONTAINS A MINI BOTTLE OF SPIRITS DISGUISED AS A DARK CHOCOLATE LOG. SHE TAKES A SWIG OF IT.

CISSIE: Really, Ada. You really are the limit.

ADA:
It's purely medicinal. For emergencies only in case of a nuclear attack and I'm sure I just heard a bomb drop. It comes in very handy in case of extreme shock.

DINER:
Waitress!

CISSIE:
All right, all right, I'm coming. He's nothing but trouble that one, he's been like that ever since he was banned from the Kardomah Cafe over that incident with the buck rarebit.

83

DINER:

Can you hear me!

CISSIE:

Oh shut it. He's not got much patience, has he.

ADA:

He'll have less once he gets a mouthful of Monsieur Henri's cooking, it's nothing but muck muck and double muck.

CISSIE:

Will you keep your voice down, someone might hear you.

ADA:

I'm not bothered. Listen, I took a doggy bag home last week, Steak Diane for out Rover. It wolfed it down then spent the entire night with its paw down its throat.

CISSIE:

(SPOTS SOMETHING OFF CAMERA) Oh look. That man over there. He seems to be having a heart attack.

ADA:

Ooh look at his face, he's gone the colour of putty. Well it's a great pity but there's not a thing we can do about it, is there.

CISSIE:
Why isn't there?

ADA:
Well it's not our table is it.

THE NEW NEIGHBOURS

ADA'S FRONT ROOM. ADA IS PEEPING OUT THROUGH THE CURTAINS AT SOMETHING THAT HAS TAKEN HER INTEREST.

ADA:
Look at next-door's whippet. It's chewing all the roots off my begonias and I only planted them in last week.....ooooh!

CISSIE:
Whatever's the matter, Ada?

ADA:
Well let's just say they've been given another dose of fertilizer. (SHOUTS AND WAVES HER HANDS) Gerroutofit and do it in your own garden you mucky devil!

CISSIE:
Has it gone?

ADA:
It's going, thank God. I'll tell you something, Cissie, I don't like the look of them new people who've moved in at number nine, they look foreign to me.

CISSIE:

Well as a matter of fact they are foreign. He's from the Levant.

ADA:

I never heard the toilet flush. He looks just like an Arab mugger. Well I wouldn't like to meet him on a dark night that's for sure.

CISSIE:

Ada, must you be so narrow-minded? We live in an age of equality; you have to bend with the wind.

ADA:

That's nearly impossible with these new corsets, it's like being in a vice. Any sudden movement I could get a whalebone through my gusset.

CISSIE:

My Leonard met him at the Town Hall yesterday and he said he was a man of extreme quality, very well educated and terribly erudite.

ADA:

Well they all are, that's why there's so many of them, it's the heat. (SHE SPOTS SOMETHING) Oh, Cissie, Cissie, over here, you don't want to be missing this.

CISSIE:
Whatever is it?

ADA:
A furniture van's started unloading more stuff. Oh, I say, they've got some lovely things. Elephant's foot ashtray. You'll get plenty fag ends in that. And there goes the three piece suite. Uncut Macaque. What are those bits of cloth dangling from the back of the settee.

CISSIE:
(SCOFFS) Bits of cloth! They're anti-macassers.

ADA:
They've got relatives staying with them, have they?

CISSIE:
Anti-macassers are decorative pieces of material! They're sort of doilies. They keep the backs of the settee nice and clean. (SHE JOINS ADA AT THE WINDOW) Oh I say, that's a nice looking pouffe.

ADA:
Which one is that, is it the big blond lad carrying the chair?

CISSIE:
That's the trouble with you, Ada, you've got a one track mind. Your Bert is just the same, he's always got sex on the brain too.

88

ADA:

I know he has, I just wish he'd lower it now and again. I'll tell you something, Cissie, he's never performed the same since he was taken prisoner in Tashkent. (SHE SPOTS SOMETHING OUTSIDE) Oh I say! Who's that young fellow? He's really handsome. I could go for him.

CISSIE:

That's their eldest son, Hassan. He's tall, isn't he.

ADA:

Very tall.

CISSIE:

And proud.

ADA:

Very proud.

CISSIE:

And that tanned, dusky colouring. Reminds you a bit of a Bedouin.

ADA:

I don't know about a bed win I bet you couldn't lose with him in bed with you.

CISSIE:

I can't argue you there, Chuck. Bless him.

ADA:

Bless him. He reminds me a bit of Rudolph Valentino.

CISSIE:

Oh yes! Galloping across the desert on his camel with his Riffs.

ADA:

I always take bicarbonate of soda when I have them, that seems to settle me.

CISSIE:

My Leonard says they're very religious, the people of the Levant.

ADA:
Oh?

CISSIE:

Apparently. He says they follow the teachings of Islam. Yes, they all want to go to Mecca.

ADA:

Well we all like a game of bingo, don't we. Oh, I say, what's that they're taking in now?

CISSIE:

Oh yes! Now that is superb. It's a gilded harp. One of them must be a harpist.

ADA:

You can't kill a whale with one of them, surely? He's walking a bit funny isn't he, a bit like my Bert when he's had one too many.

CISSIE:

He's a disgrace to the neighbourhood that husband of yours. I'd like to know what's driving him to drink.

ADA:

A taxi when he can afford it, otherwise the 73 bus, stops right outside the pub

CISSIE:

I mean what good is he to you, Ada. He hasn't worked since the end of the war; he just sits at home all day with a bottle in his hand.

ADA:

Well he's got to take it out of his mouth some of the time.

CISSIE:

You mark my words, your husband will finish up in penury.

ADA

No, he always drinks in the Dog and Duck. He's very friendly with the landlord, if Bert loses his teeth he lets him suck the beer mats.

CISSIE:

I mean the fellers you could have had, Ada. Fred Pickles for one.

ADA:

I remember Fred, little feller with a moustache. Yes I liked Fred. Took me out often. He tried to....you know he tried it on with me.

CISSIE:

I hope you kept your hand on your ha'penny.

ADA:

I had enough hands on it to cover up two and sixpence.

CISSIE:

I can't blame you.

ADA:

He was a big football fan, you know. He watched all the teams, United, City, even Stockport County. In those days I was going in for advanced cooking, I remember.

CISSIE:

Cordon Bleu?

ADA:

Some of my stuff should have been cordoned off. So I just stuck meat and mashed potatoes usually. And I took Fred home for a meal one night when my mam and dad were out. Chicken, but unfortunately the dog had eaten all of it but the back end so I just used that and hoped he wouldn't notice. I called it Football Supporter Chicken Kiev.

CISSIE:
And did he like it?

ADA:
Well I don't really know but he never watched Arsenal again.

AT THE LAUNDRETTE

CISSIE IS WAITING FOR THE WASHING CYCLE TO END. ADA COMES IN WITH HER SHOPPING TROLLEY OF DIRTY WASHING, SITS DOWN BESIDE CISSIE.

CISSIE:
Oh, hello Chuck. You're a bit late, I'm already on my second spin. (SHE NOTICES THAT ADA IS IN TEARS) What's the matter, Ada, what's upset you.

ADA:
(TAKES OUT AN OUTSIZE HANDKERCHIEF AND DRIES HER TEARS) I'm filling up, Cissie.

CISSIE:
I can see that, but why?

ADA:
I keep remembering Doris Plumstead's funeral. I was in the kitchen making the tea when I found out she'd gone. I'd got my mince on regulo 120, and I was just braising Bert's sprouts - because he's always like his sprouts braised, has Bert - when little Elsie from number 27, you know her with the very bad acne, looks like she's been pebble-dashed, came in and told me the news.

CISSIE:
Tragic, wasn't it.

ADA:
She was a lovely woman, Doris. A nicer body never broke a day's bread. That woman was a heroine, you know. During the First World War she drove an ambulance for the French through the Ardennes. She was awarded the Crotch de Gaulle. She liked the men you know, Doris Plumstead. She had more soldiers than Kitchener. She was ninety-eight when she went, you know.

CISSIE:
Well it's a good age, isn't it. Who did the teas after her funeral?

ADA:
The Gardenia Cafe.

CISSIE:
Very nice. Did they push the boat out and have tongue?

ADA:
Oh yes, there was some tongue. Of course I never eat tongue.

CISSIE:
Oh I like a bit of tongue. Why don't you like it?

ADA:

I just don't. I refuse to eat anything that comes out of an animal's mouth.

CISSIE:

So what did you have then?

ADA:

An egg.

CISSIE:

Who did the internment for her?

ADA:

Well that was a surprise because I thought Potter's in Johnson Street would be doing it. Because they always do a good job. Well they put our Jack down last year and we haven't seen him since. So help me God, Cissie, I couldn't believe it; the Co-op buried him.

CISSIE:

(PULLS A FACE) The Co-op?

ADA:

Cheap, cheap, cheap. I couldn't believe it, Cissie. They only did it for the divi. I said to Mavis: 'How dare you bury your mother in a pine coffin?'

CISSIE:

They never put her in *pine*!

ADA:

I said to their Mavis she's only got to stretch her arms and the sides will collapse. I think that's what brought this on, you know. And if that isn't all my back's bad again and I've got clusters of varicose veins on my knees. I've seen less blue veins on a stilton cheese. As soon as Elsie told me I felt a flush coming on. I held on to the architrave of the door. She's expecting again you know, Mavis.

CISSIE:
No!

ADA:

Yes, she's impregnable again. Do you know, this is her seventh?

CISSIE:
Good Heavens, she'd hardly time to draw breath.

ADA:

It was like shelling peas with her. She's carried more water than the Mekon Delta.

CISSIE:
The poor woman.

ADA:

Well I tried talking to her. And talking to him is even worse. Well there's no need for me to tell you what these
97

Hungarian acrobats are like. He never leaves her alone. It's paw, paw, paw all the time with him. A snatch of The Blue Danube and he's on her. I put it down to the chemical works.

CISSIE:
Oh?

ADA:
Yes, he works there as a research chemist.

CISSIE:
Oh I didn't know that.

ADA:
Oh yes, he's on superannuation. My Bert is working there temporary as a janitor at the research lab, sweeping up. And apparently they've been experimenting with a high fertility pill for important goats.

CISSIE:
You mean to make them....perform, like.

ADA:
Yes.

CISSIE:
What are they like, these pills?

ADA:

I don't know but Bert says they taste a bit like peppermint.

THE DRIER STOPS AND CISSIE TAKES OUT OF IT A PAIR OF JODPHURS.

CISSIE:

I don't want to let these get too dry.

ADA:

So help me God, surgical knickers. I didn't know you had to wear them, Cissie? You've not got that trouble again, have you?

CISSIE:

Don't be silly, these are jodphurs. They belong to out Jocelyn. She's recently moved to Knutsford, she's going round with the upper set now.

ADA:

Doesn't she bother with her bottom set now then?

CISSIE:

You really are ignorant you know, Ada.

ADA:

Well she always had trouble with her teeth, I remember.

CISSIE:

That's because from time to time she had a touch of pyhorrhea.

ADA:

She must have had too much roughage in her diet. (SHE STARTS REMOVING HER DIRTY WASHING FROM HER TROLLEY) I'll sort my washing out now. (SHE PRODUCES A VERY LARGE PAIR OF PINK KNICKERS)

CISSIE:

I bet you can't turn your Bert on with those.

ADA:

I couldn't turn him on with a starting handle. I'll tell you something, shall I?

CISSIE:

I'm all ears.

ADA:

He hasn't....you know....since V.E. Day. We'd lit a bonfire to celebrate the end of the war. He ignited a rocket and the jam jar fell over. The rocket went right up the leg of his trousers. It took four of us to get him down from the tree. He was lay there sprawled out in the uppermost branches. Impaled on weather cones. We went willy-nilly to the infirmary. One of the cones was too deeply embedded. That weather cone is still there. It comes in handy though. We can always tell when it's going to rain.

****

Television repeats of Les's work are few and far between, so perhaps these Cissie & Ada scripts, which were brought wonderfully to life by Les and Roy, will go a little way towards filling the void he left. I hope you enjoy reading them as much as I enjoyed writing them. Some of the sketches in this book can be viewed in their entirety on YouTube. Other, for some reason, have only been uploaded in part. For example the first two or three minutes of The Art Gallery sketch are missing. Not to worry, you've seen it here.

Terry Ravenscroft, June 2020.

An extract from Terry Ravenscroft's latest novel, Jerry's, which Cissie and Ada would no doubt find more than a bit *risqué*.

Near the bottom end of Moors Road, Throgley's main thoroughfare that split the village into more or less equal halves, a sign outside the front door of the small detached whitewashed cottage stated that Ellen Summerfield D.P.M. Podiatrist could be found within. Roses round the door, something of a novelty in Throgley, perhaps brought with them a little comfort to those clients who might perhaps have to go through a little pain in the process of having their ingrown toenails and suchlike attended to.

Behind the front door, in fact behind the bedroom door, Nell, as Ellen now preferred to be called, was going about her profession with customary diligence.

"How would you like me?" she said coyly to the pleasant-looking man, a walk-in, not one of her usual clients. She scolded herself. "Oh I'm sorry, whatever am I thinking of, I forgot to ask your name?"

"Harkness. Mr Harkness. Brian."

"I'll call you Brian shall I? Less formal. She smiled, cocking her head to one side appealingly like a cocker spaniel persuading its owner to take it for a walk. "If that's all right with you?"

"Yes. Yes of course."

"I'm Nell." She regarded him, a little concerned. "You seem a bit shy, Brian. Is it your first time perhaps?"

"First time? I wish," he said with a grimace. "No, I see a lady in Bristol. Where I hail from." He gave a wry smile. "However she doesn't seem to be doing me much good."

"*I'll* do you some good, Brian."

Pleased at her confidence Harkness nodded. "Good. Excellent. You see I've seen all of Jerry's I want to see....and I've half-an-hour to fill in before the coach moves on....so I thought why not?"

"Why not indeed?"

Nell, propped up on an elbow, her head crooked in the palm of her hand, was reclining on the purple duvet of a big, pink silk-canopied four-poster bed. The flock-wallpapered room was redolent of expensive perfume, the lighting subdued, the temperature cosy. She crooked a finger and beckoned him invitingly. "Join me, Brian, please. No need to be shy."

A bit puzzled at the welcome, but not one to make a fuss, Harkness stepped over to the bed. He had not thought it at all odd when the podiatrist had led him upstairs - after all, Mr Davies the osteopath he saw for his bad back carried out his practice on the first floor of his home and there was nothing unusual in that. And he had only been mildly surprised by the podiatrist's décolleté, sheer black stockings and high leather boots: if she did a good job who was he to criticise the clothes she chose to work in; she was a pretty woman, pretty women liked to enhance their prettiness. As for the bed, well he had to lie down at the osteopaths, people lay down when visiting a psychiatrist too; perhaps she could do a better job if the patient was prone?

Nell patted the space on the bed beside her invitingly. "Sit."

Harkness sat.

She rewarded him with another smile and touched him lightly on the shoulder, letting it linger there limpet-like. "That's better."

"Shall I take my shoes off?" Harkness asked.

"What?"

"My shoes. And socks. I'll take them off shall I?"

Nell shrugged noncommittally and put the rosy red-nippled breast that had fought its way loose during the shrugging back where it belonged. "Well if you like. Whatever turns you...." It suddenly dawned on her. "Oh my! You're a *foot fetishist!* " She clapped her hands together in delight. "I've never had a foot fetishist before." She rubbed her hands together and with an eager smile rolled up imaginary sleeves. "What would you like me to do with them? Give them a titty roll?"

Harkness gaped at her. "W....what?"

"Put them between my tits and give them a good squeezing?" She clasped the sides of her breasts, pushed them together and rolled them round and round in demonstration.

Harkness was much concerned. "Wouldn't that do more harm than good?"

"What?"

"Well I can't see that curing my bunions."

A second later the penny dropped. Nell grinned hugely. "You think I'm a podiatrist, don't you!"

"Well of course."

She shook her head. "Sorry. Sorry, Brian." She reproached herself. "I really must take that sign down." She smiled another apology. "I thought you knew. I thought everyone knew nowadays."

At one time Nell would have treated Harkness's bunions and been glad to. But one day about six months ago she was still in bed fast asleep following a glass of prosecco too much the night before when the ringing of her front doorbell heralded her first, in fact her only customer of the day, and she had hurriedly answered the door whilst still in her nightgown. The nightgown was flimsy, Nell overfilled the top part of it enough to cause excitement, the rest of her body was far from unattractive, her face pretty. Her customer, a Mr Martin from Wormhole, helped himself to an eyeful of her charms and by the time he left an hour later a lot more than his claw toe had been attended to.

At the time in question business was as slow as it had ever been - there being another, more established podiatry practice in the village didn't help. It was a situation Nell thought she would be able to handle on setting up her practice a year previously but had soon found to her cost that she couldn't. Her tryst with Mr Martin was the catalyst that got her to thinking a better living might be made ministering to men's sexual needs rather than their feet. It was, and by now Nell never even gave podiatry a thought, far less practised it. She was making a fortune. Soon after Mr Martin's visit quite a few males in Throgley and the neighbouring villages suddenly discovered they had something wrong with their feet. Business boomed. It boomed even more when visitors to the village got to hear about it - Nell making it her business to absolutely ensure they heard about it by giving a couple of her local clients a free one per week in turn for informing male tourists who fancied a memory of their visit to Throgley and its Sir Jerrold Wainwright Memorial Public Convenience other than those they could get at the gift shop and village tours.

A regular client had once remarked, whilst climbing back into his clothes, that while he was more than happy with the way she had chosen to make a living didn't she sometimes think it had been rather a waste of time and money to spend three years at university learning how to be a podiatrist when she had ended up doing what she did? The waste never bothered at Nell at all. Many people went to university to study something or other and ended up doing something else. People studied architecture and became merchant bankers, people studied medicine and became comedians, people studied all manner of subjects and became Tesco shelf stackers, if only on a, hopefully, temporary basis. Besides, like lots of others, she was doing something she had learned to do at university. Fuck lots of different men very often.

"How much do you charge?" said Harkness tentatively.

"Forty pounds straight, sixty pounds anything you want, and I'll throw in a shufty at your bunions for free."

Printed in Great Britain
by Amazon